TV **COOKS**

Mary Berry

COOKS

Cakes

Photographs by Juliet Piddington

BBC BOOKS

Published by BBC Books,
an imprint of BBC Worldwide Limited,
Woodlands, 80 Wood Lane, London W12 0TT.

The recipes in this book first appeared in:
Mary Berry's Quick & Easy Cakes
© Mary Berry 1993
Mary Berry's Ultimate Cake Book
© Mary Berry 1994

This edition first published 1998
Recipes © Mary Berry 1998
The moral right of the author has been asserted
Photographs by Juliet Piddington © BBC Consumer
Publishing 1998
Author photograph by John Jefford © BBC Consumer
Publishing 1998

ISBN 0 563 38411 5

Edited by Pam Mallender
Designed by Sarah Amit
Styling by Marian Price
Home Economist: Sarah Ramsbottom

Set in New Caledonia and Helvetica
Printed and bound in France by Imprimerie Pollina s.a.
Colour separations by Imprimerie Pollina s.a.
Cover printed by Imprimerie Pollina s.a.

Cover and frontispiece: Sunday Best Chocolate Fudge Cake

CONTENTS

RECIPE NOTES

Eggs are medium (formerly size 3) unless otherwise specified. If your kitchen is warm, keep the eggs in the fridge, but allow them to come to room temperature before using. While the proven risks of healthy people becoming ill from eating fresh raw eggs is minimal, pregnant women, the sick, the elderly and the very young should not do so just in case.

Spoon measurements are level. Always use proper measuring spoons: 1 teaspoon = 5ml and 1 tablespoon = 15ml.

Never mix metric or imperial measures in one recipe. Stick to one or the other.

HANDY CONVERSION TABLES

Weight		Volume		Linear	
15g	½oz	30ml	1fl oz	5mm	¼in
25g	1oz	50ml	2fl oz	10mm/1cm	½in
40g	1½oz	100ml	3½fl oz	2cm	¾in
55g	2oz	125ml	4fl oz	2.5cm	1in
85g	3oz	150ml	5fl oz (¼ pint)	5cm	2in
115g	4oz	175ml	6fl oz	7.5cm	3in
140g	5oz	200ml	7fl oz (⅓ pint)	10cm	4in
175g	6oz	225ml	8fl oz	13cm	5in
200g	7oz	250ml	9fl oz	15cm	6in
225g	8oz	300ml	10fl oz (½ pint)	18cm	7in
250g	9oz	350ml	12fl oz	20cm	8in
280g	10oz	400ml	14fl oz	23cm	9in
350g	12oz	425ml	15fl oz (¾ pint)	25cm	10in
375g	13oz	450ml	16fl oz	28cm	11in
400g	14oz	500ml	18fl oz	30cm	12in
425g	15oz	600ml	20fl oz (1 pint)		
450g	1lb	700ml	1¼ pints		
550g	1¼lb	850ml	1½ pints		
750g	1lb 10oz	1 litre	1¾ pints		
900g	2lb	1.2 litres	2 pints		
1kg	2¼lb	1.3 litres	2¼ pints		
1.3kg	3lb	1.4 litres	2½ pints		
1.8kg	4lb	1.7 litres	3 pints		
2.25kg	5lb	2 litres	3½ pints		
		2.5 litres	4½ pints		

Oven temperatures

225F	110C	GAS ¼
250F	120C	GAS ½
275F	140C	GAS 1
300F	150C	GAS 2
325F	160C	GAS 3
350F	180C	GAS 4
375F	190C	GAS 5
400F	200C	GAS 6
425F	220C	GAS 7
450F	230C	GAS 8
475F	240C	GAS 9

�"f" **Low fat**

❋ **Suitable for freezing**

I have always enjoyed baking – I love to have something special in the cake tin for my family and friends. Techniques have changed greatly since I first began baking: cake making has never been simpler. The new all-in-one method is amazingly easy. Just measure the ingredients into the bowl – usually eggs, soft baking magarine, self-raising flour, sugar, plus a little baking powder – beat until smooth by hand or machine and it's done. Perfect for sponges and traybakes.

Many of the cakes in this book freeze well. For best results, freeze them straight away when they are fresh. If they are fairly plain just wrap them in foil or plastic film and freeze. Even iced cakes freeze though you may find they lose a little of their shine on thawing if they are already decorated. Open-freeze iced cakes overnight until firm. Then wrap in foil, place in a polythene container or cardboard box and label. Most cakes should be thawed at room temperature for 8 hours before serving although small cakes take less time. If you've made a cake for the weekend and you have some left that you don't want to eat right away, freeze individual slices and add them to a lunch box or use for a picnic.

Do remember when baking that all ovens vary – cakes bake more quickly in an electric fan-oven and so you may have to reduce my suggested temperatures. Cakes might burn near the back of some small gas ovens so again you may have to reduce my temperatures. Always consult the manufacturer's instruction book that comes with the cooker and, if you have an AGA, consult *The AGA Book* for specific baking instructions.

I do hope you will enjoy baking these cakes as much as your friends and family will enjoy eating them!

Mary Berry.

INGREDIENTS

Apricot jam
This is invaluable for brushing a cake that is to be iced. Gently heat the jam to make it runny, then strain to remove any lumps if it is for a special occasion. Brush over the cake, where it will 'set' and prevent any stray crumbs working their way into the icing. Neither will the icing become dull; with the apricot layer in between, the moisture in the icing won't be absorbed by the cake. The jam also acts as a 'glue' to help almond paste stick.

Baking powder
This is the raising agent most commonly added in cake making. It consists of an acid (usually cream of tartar) and an alkali (bicarbonate of soda) mixed with dried starch or flour. When moistened the chemicals react to produce carbon dioxide which expands during baking, making the cake rise. The baking powders on the market today contain a slower-acting raising agent which is more tolerant if mixtures are made up and left. If it is more convenient, make up the cake mixture, then bake it later. Don't be tempted to add more than the recipe specifies or the mixture will rise well at first but will then collapse, resulting in a heavy, close-textured cake.

Butter
It is not always necessary to use butter to obtain the best results, but it must be used where a buttery flavour is all-important, for instance in scones. I tend to use a salted or lightly salted butter – the unsalted kind is far too expensive! The temperature of butter is crucial to the success of a cake mix. It needs to be taken out of the fridge and left at room temperature for at least 30 minutes before it is used in a creaming method. Even then it is often better to cream the butter alone to soften it further before adding the sugar.

Fruit and nuts
Most dried fruit now comes ready washed, but it is wise to quickly pick over the fruit to remove any small pieces of stalk. The fruit can dry out once the packet is opened, so store in an airtight container, or freeze in polythene bags to keep the maximum flavour. Nuts are expensive and have a short shelf life, quickly going rancid in a warm kitchen. Use the freezer as an extra store cupboard, or keep small quantities in airtight containers, preferably in the fridge. Whole shelled nuts keep for up to five years in the freezer, flaked and ground almonds for one year. Shake out only what is required and pop the remainder back.

Golden syrup and black treacle
These are made from selected refinery liquor after the refined sugar has been crystallized. Golden syrup is light and sweet; treacle, which has added cane molasses, is very much darker and stronger.

Margarine
Soft margarines have greatly improved and now have a good flavour. Cakes made with them have excellent keeping qualities and they are very useful for the all-in-one method. Always check the packet and avoid low-fat spreads – their high water content makes them unsuitable for cake making. Hard or block margarines vary in degrees of hardness. Look for those specifically labelled for baking. These are best used for the melting or rubbed-in methods.

Spices
Ready-blended spices, such as ground mixed spice, are useful to have for general flavouring, but some recipes call for individual spices such as ground cinnamon, ginger and cloves. All spices should be as fresh as possible, and have an even better flavour when freshly ground. Buy spices in small quantities and replace often. Store in the dark. Buy whole nutmegs in particular to grate freshly when needed. Stem ginger is useful in a few recipes. If you like the flavour use the ginger itself and the syrup lavishly!

Sugar

I like to use the more natural sugars such as golden caster and golden granulated sugar – they have so much more flavour – but there is now a huge variety of sugars and sweeteners available which can add different textures and some interesting flavours.

Caster: this is the one most commonly used. Its small regular grain ensures that it blends smoothly to give an even texture to whisked sponges, creamed mixtures and meringues.

Granulated: this has a coarser texture than caster and is best used for rubbed-in cake mixtures or in melting methods. If used in a creamed mixture it will give a slight grittiness and a speckled appearance to the cake.

Icing: this is not generally used for basic cake mixtures as its fine sugar crystals produce poor volume and a hard crust. It is essential to use it in cake icings, although we now have the option of buying ready-made royal icing.

Muscovado: traditionally made from raw cane sugar, the colour and flavour vary according to the molasses content. Light muscovado is excellent in many cakes as it creams well and has a lovely caramel flavour. Dark muscovado easily overpowers other flavours and needs to be used with care. It gives an excellent colour and flavour to gingerbreads and rich fruit cakes.

Demerara: this is traditionally unrefined and is most suitable for cakes made by the melting method where heat and moisture dissolve its large crystals. It is also useful for sprinkling on top of cakes.

EQUIPMENT

Baking trays and cake tins

At least three baking trays are essential. They should be flat, rigid and heavy. Good quality, strong, solid cake tins are worth the initial investment and will last you a lifetime. If you opt for non-stick ones, it is still wise to follow the recipe instructions for greasing and lining and not rely solely on the tin's non-stick properties. The correct size tin is of paramount importance while the depth is particularly important for sponge cakes. Sandwich tins should preferably be non-stick and loose-bottomed. A roasting tin is ideal for traybakes.

Whisks and mixers

An electric whisk is essential to the all-in-one method of cake making, although it doesn't matter whether it is hand-held or an electric food mixer. A wire balloon whisk is also useful for small quantities of egg yolks, egg whites and cream. A food processor is very much a time saver, but it is all too easy to over-process a mixture. Use the pulse button where available to give you more control.

Knives

A palette knife is indispensable to spread and smooth mixtures into tins or icings on to cakes, as well as to lift biscuits off baking trays or loosen a cake from the sides of the tin before turning out. You'll also need a long, sharp serrated knife to cut a cake cleanly. You'll find a fish slice useful for lifting out traybakes.

Skewers

Long, thin metal skewers are vital for testing when a cake is done. They should be flattened not spiral. If you don't have skewers use the point of a long, thin sharp knife.

Wire racks

You should have at least two for cooling cakes once they have been baked. Round ones are available, but large rectangular ones are better. Or you can, of course, use the rack from your grill pan.

1. Apricot jam
2. Black treacle
3. Nibbed sugar
4. Almond paste
5. Chocolate
6. Cocoa
7. Icing sugar
8. Golden syrup
9. Almond essence
10. Vanilla essence
11. Coffee essence
12. Caster sugar
13. Oats
14. Glacé cherries
15. Apricots
16. Sunflower seeds
17. Blueberries
18. Citron peel
19. Banana chips
20. Currants
21. Sultanas
22. Raisins
23. Light muscovado sugar
24. Dark muscovado sugar
25. Demerara sugar
26. Soft margarine
27. Hard margarine

1 Baking trays
2 Ring mould
3 Measuring jug
4 Wire racks
5 Loaf tin
6 Shallow square tin
7 Roasting tin
8 Dariole moulds
9 Skewers
10 Palette knife
11 Sugar thermometer
12 Pastry brush
13 Wooden spoons
14 Fairy-cake paper cases
15 Bun tin
16 Measuring spoons
17 Muffin tin
18 Piping nozzles
19 Muffin paper cases

Chocolate Cakes

SUNDAY BEST CHOCOLATE FUDGE CAKE

This cake is ideal for Sunday afternoon tea. To make it even more special, do take time to heat a little apricot jam to brush over it before icing. This keeps the cake moist.

Cuts into 8 wedges

25g/1oz cocoa powder

3 tbsp boiling water

175g/6oz soft margarine

175g/6oz caster sugar

3 large eggs

175g/6oz self-raising flour

1½tsp baking powder

warmed apricot jam (optional)

chocolate curls (See Tip), flake or grated chocolate, to decorate

FOR THE FUDGE ICING

55g/2oz hard margarine

25g/1oz cocoa powder, sifted

about 2 tbsp milk

225g/8oz icing sugar, sifted

1 Preheat the oven to 180C/350F/Gas 4. Grease and base line two 18cm/7in sandwich tins with greased greaseproof paper.

2 Blend the cocoa with the boiling water, to make a paste, in a large bowl and leave to cool. Add the margarine, sugar, eggs, flour and baking powder to the bowl and beat thoroughly for 1–2 minutes. Divide the mixture between the tins and bake for 25–30 minutes or until the cakes have shrunk slightly from the sides of the tins and they spring back when pressed lightly with a finger. Turn out, remove the lining papers and leave to cool on a wire rack.

3 Make the icing: melt the margarine in a small pan, add the cocoa powder and cook for 1 minute. Remove from the heat and stir in the milk and icing sugar. Beat well until smooth. Cool a little until the icing is of spreading consistency.

4 Spread a little jam, if using, on to the top of one of the cakes (this will be the middle of the cake) and top with half the fudge icing. Place the remaining cake on top, brush with jam, if using, and top with the remaining fudge icing, warmed if necessary. Decorate with chocolate curls or scrolls (See Tip), flake or grated chocolate.

Nutrition notes per serving: *554 calories, Protein 6g, Carbohydrate 72g, Fat 29g, Saturated fat 7g, Fibre 1g, Added sugar 53g, Salt 1.25g.*

TIP

For chocolate curls: Scrape a vegetable peeler along the flat side of a chilled chocolate bar.

For *caraque* or scrolls: Melt chocolate-flavoured cake covering (not a patch on the real thing, but far easier to handle) in a heatproof bowl over a pan of gently simmering water. Pour a thin layer onto a scratchproof surface, spread thinly with a palette knife and leave until it begins to set and go cloudy. When it no longer sticks to your hand when you touch it, shave the chocolate off the surface using a long, sharp flexible knife to form *caraque* or scrolls.

MARBLED CHOCOLATE RING CAKE

This family weekend cake has a nice texture and looks spectacular, marbled with white and brown. It must be eaten fresh.

Cuts into 10 slices

225g/8oz soft margarine

225g/8oz caster sugar

4 eggs

225g/8oz self-raising flour

2 tsp baking powder

1½ tbsp cocoa

1½ tbsp hot water

FOR THE ICING

140g/5oz plain chocolate, broken into pieces

115g/4oz butter, diced

55g/2oz milk chocolate, broken into pieces

1 Preheat the oven to 180C/350F/Gas 4. Lightly grease a 1.7 litre/3 pint capacity ring mould.

2 Place all the cake ingredients, apart from the cocoa and hot water, in a large bowl. Beat well until thoroughly blended. Using a teaspoon, dot about half of this mixture into the base of the tin.

3 In a small bowl, mix together the cocoa and hot water, then mix into the remaining cake mixture. Dot this mixture over and between the teaspoons of plain mixture until it is all used up. Swirl a little with a knife, then carefully level the surface.

4 Bake for 40 minutes or until well risen and springy to the touch. Allow to cool in the tin for a few minutes before turning out. Leave to cool completely on a wire rack.

5 Make the icing: melt the plain chocolate slowly in a heatproof bowl with two tablespoons of water and the butter over a pan of simmering, not boiling, water. Pour over the cake and leave to set for about 1 hour.

6 Melt the milk chocolate slowly in a heatproof bowl over a pan of simmering, not boiling, water. Spoon into a paper piping bag (See Tip), cut off the tip of the bag and drizzle over the top of the plain chocolate icing. Leave to set.

Nutrition notes per serving: *554 calories, Protein 6g, Carbohydrate 54g, Fat 36g, Saturated fat 14g, Fibre 1g, Added sugar 35g, Salt 1.27g.*

TIP

A quick and easy way to pipe chocolate is to place the melted chocolate into two small polythene bags which have been put inside each other for strength. Snip off one corner, then simply drizzle the chocolate over the cake.

DEVIL'S FOOD CAKE

This classic American cake is moist and dark, and slightly bitter in flavour. The frosting is very sweet, though, crisp on the top and like marshmallow underneath. Proper American frosting requires the use of a sugar thermometer. Use the 'instant' recipe (See Tip) if you don't have a sugar thermometer, or simply for speed.

Cuts into 8 wedges

55g/2oz cocoa

115g/4oz soft margarine

280g/10oz caster sugar

2 eggs, lightly whisked

175g/6oz plain flour

¼ tsp baking powder

1 tsp bicarbonate of soda

FOR THE AMERICAN FROSTING

450g/1lb caster sugar

2 egg whites

1 Preheat the oven to 180C/350F/Gas 4. Grease and base line two 20cm/8in sandwich tins with greased greaseproof paper.

2 Whisk the cocoa into 225ml/8fl oz water until smooth and set aside. Place the margarine in a bowl, gradually whisk in the sugar until the mixture is pale and fluffy, then gradually whisk in the eggs until evenly blended.

3 Sift the flour, baking powder and bicarbonate of soda together and fold into the creamed mixture alternately with the cocoa and water. Divide between the tins and level the surface. Bake for 30–45 minutes or until well risen and firm to the touch. Allow to cool in the tins for a few minutes, then turn out, remove the lining papers and leave to cool completely on a wire rack.

4 Make the American frosting: place the sugar in a large heavy-based pan with 135ml/4½fl oz water and heat gently until the sugar has dissolved. Bring to the boil and boil until it registers 115C/240F on a sugar thermometer.

5 Whisk the egg whites in a large, deep heatproof bowl until stiff. Allow the syrup bubbles to settle, then slowly pour the hot syrup on to the egg whites, whisking constantly. When all the syrup has been added, continue whisking until the mixture stands in peaks and just starts to become matt around the edges.

6 Sandwich the cakes together with a little of the frosting. Spread the remainder over the top and sides, using a palette knife. Pull the frosting up into peaks all over. Work quickly as the icing sets rapidly. Leave to set in a cool place, but not in the fridge.

Nutrition notes per serving: *583 calories, Protein 6g, Carbohydrate 114g, Fat 15g, Saturated fat 4g, Fibre 1g, Added sugar 96g, Salt 1.01g.*

TIP

For an 'instant' American frosting: place 175g/6oz caster sugar, one egg white, two tablespoons of hot water and a pinch of cream of tartar in a heatproof bowl over a pan of simmering, not boiling, water. Whisk for 10–12 minutes until thick. Use immediately to fill and ice the cake.

AMERICAN CHOCOLATE MUFFINS ✳

115g/4oz plain chocolate, broken into pieces

115g/4oz walnuts, roughly chopped

225g/8oz self-raising flour

1 tsp baking powder

25g/1oz cocoa, sifted

175g/6oz caster sugar

200ml/7fl oz milk

4 tbsp sunflower oil

1 large egg

1 Preheat the oven to 220C/425F/Gas 7. Lightly grease 12 deep muffin tins if you are using ordinary fairy cake paper cases, as the mixture will rise well above the paper cases, and place the paper cases in the tins (See Tip). You do not need to grease the tins if muffin paper cases are used.

2 Melt the chocolate in a large heatproof bowl over a pan of simmering, not boiling, water. Remove from the heat and beat in the remaining ingredients. Spoon into the cases and bake for 15–20 minutes, or until well risen and firm to the touch. Serve warm.

Nutrition notes per serving: *294 calories, Protein 5g, Carbohydrate 37g, Fat 15g, Saturated fat 4g, Fibre 1g, Added sugar 21g, Salt 0.37g.*

✳ *These freeze well. Simply defrost, warm through in a hot oven, then serve.*

TIP

Use deep mince-pie tins if you don't have proper muffin tins.

CHOCOLATE CHIP BROWNIES

175g/6oz unsalted butter, diced

175g/6oz plain chocolate, broken into pieces

125g/4½oz self-raising flour

350g/12oz light muscovado sugar

4 eggs, lightly beaten

85g/3oz milk chocolate chips

1 Preheat the oven to 180C/350F/Gas 4. Grease and base line a 30x23cm/12x9in roasting tin with greased greaseproof paper.

2 Melt the butter and chocolate in a heatproof bowl over a pan of simmering, not boiling, water, then cool slightly. In a large bowl, mix together the flour, sugar and eggs and add the chocolate mixture. Stir well until thoroughly blended. Add the chocolate chips.

3 Pour the mixture into the tin and bake for 45–50 minutes or until just firm to the touch. Cool in the tin and cut into squares to serve. Lift out using a palette knife.

Nutrition notes per serving: *237 calories, Protein 3g, Carbohydrate 31g, Fat 12g, Saturated fat 7g, Fibre trace, Added sugar 26g, Salt 0.11g.*

Traybakes

BASIC ALL-IN-ONE SPONGE TRAYBAKE

Cuts into 21 squares

225g/8oz soft margarine

225g/8oz caster sugar

280g/10oz self-raising flour

2 tsp baking powder

4 eggs

4 tbsp milk

1 Preheat the oven to 180C/350F/Gas 4. Grease and base line a 30x23cm/12x9in roasting tin with greased greaseproof paper. Alternatively, line the tin with non-stick baking paper or greased foil.

2 Place all the ingredients in a large bowl and beat well for 2 minutes or until well blended. Transfer to the tin and level the top.

3 Bake for 35–40 minutes or until the cake has shrunk from the sides of the tin and springs back when pressed in the centre with your fingertips. Leave to cool in the tin, then cut into squares. Lift out using a palette knife.

Nutrition notes per serving: *182 calories, Protein 3g, Carbohydrate 22g, Fat 10g, Saturated fat 2g, Fibre trace, Added sugar 11g, Salt 0.49g.*

SULTANA AND ORANGE TRAYBAKE

Cuts into 21 squares

225g/8oz soft margarine

225g/8oz caster sugar

280g/10oz self-raising flour

2 tsp baking powder

4 eggs

2 tbsp milk

280g/10oz sultanas

grated rind of 2 oranges

demerara sugar (See Tip)

1 Preheat the oven to 180C/350F/Gas 4. Grease and base line a 30x23cm/12x9in roasting tin with greased greaseproof paper. Alternatively, line the tin with non-stick baking paper or greased foil.

2 Place all the ingredients, except for the demerera sugar, in a large bowl and beat well for 2 minutes or until well blended. Transfer to the tin and level the top.

3 Bake for 25 minutes, then sprinkle the top with sugar and return to the oven for 10–15 minutes or until the cake has shrunk from the sides of the tin and springs back when pressed in the centre with your fingertips. Leave to cool in the tin, then cut into squares. Lift out using a palette knife.

Nutrition notes per serving: *218 calories, Protein 3g, Carbohydrate 31g, Fat 10g, Saturated fat 2g, Fibre trace, Added sugar 11g, Salt 0.50g.*

TIP

You can omit the demerara sugar and ice the cake, when it is cold, with an orange glacé icing. To make this, mix together about three tablespoons fresh orange juice and 225g/8oz sifted icing sugar until runny. Spread out evenly over the cake after it has cooled and before it is cut into squares, using a palette knife. Leave to set, then cut the cake into squares.

TREACLE SPICE TRAYBAKE

Cuts into 15–20 squares

225g/8oz soft margarine

175g/6oz caster sugar

225g/8oz black treacle

280g/10oz self-raising flour

2 tsp baking powder

2 tsp mixed spice

4 large eggs

4 tbsp milk

FOR THE ICING

85g/3oz icing sugar, sifted

2 tbsp stem ginger syrup from a jar

2 pieces stem ginger, finely chopped

1 Preheat the oven to 180C/350F/Gas 4. Grease and base line a 30x23cm/12x9in roasting tin with greased greaseproof paper. Alternatively, line the tin with non-stick baking paper or greased foil.

2 Place all the cake ingredients in a large bowl and beat well for 2 minutes or until well blended. Transfer to the tin and level the top.

3 Bake for 40 minutes or until the cake has shrunk from the sides of the tin and springs back when pressed in the centre with your fingertips. Leave to cool in the tin.

4 Make the icing: mix together the icing sugar and syrup, pour over the cake and sprinkle with the chopped stem ginger. Leave to set, then cut the cake into squares and lift out using a palette knife.

Nutrition notes per serving for 15: *319 calories, Protein 4g, Carbohydrate 46g, Fat 14g, Saturated fat 3g, Fibre trace, Added sugar 31g, Salt 0.75g.*

COFFEE FUDGE SQUARES

Cuts into 21 squares

175g/6oz soft margarine

175g/6oz caster sugar

225g/8oz self-raising flour

1½ tsp baking powder

3 eggs

2 tbsp milk

1 tbsp coffee essence (See Tip)

FOR THE FUDGE TOPPING

55g/2oz butter

115g/4oz light muscovado sugar

2 tbsp milk

280g/10oz icing sugar, sifted

25g/1oz chopped walnuts

1 Preheat the oven to 180C/350F/Gas 4. Grease and base line a 30x23cm/12x9in roasting tin with greased greaseproof paper. Alternatively, line the tin with non-stick baking paper or greased foil.

2 Place all the cake ingredients in a large bowl and beat well for 2 minutes or until well blended. Transfer to the tin and level the top.

3 Bake for 30–35 minutes or until the cake has shrunk from the sides of the tin and springs back when pressed in the centre with your fingertips. Leave to cool in the tin.

4 Make the fudge topping: place the butter, sugar and milk in a small pan and heat gently until the sugar dissolves, then boil briskly for 3 minutes. Remove from the heat and gradually stir in the icing sugar. Beat thoroughly until smooth. Spread quickly over the top of the cake and sprinkle over the walnuts. Leave to set, then cut the cake into squares and lift out using a palette knife.

Nutrition notes per serving: *244 calories, Protein 2g, Carbohydrate 37g, Fat 11g, Saturated fat 3g, Fibre trace, Added sugar 29g, Salt 0.43g.*

TIP

While it is best to use coffee essence in terms of flavour and colour, you can substitute two teaspoons instant coffee dissolved in one tablespoon of hot water for each tablespoon of coffee essence.

CHERRY AND APRICOT TRAYBAKE

Cuts into 21 squares

175g/6oz butter, softened

175g/6oz caster sugar

225g/8oz self-raising flour

1½ tsp baking powder

3 eggs

3 tbsp milk

85g/3oz glacé cherries, quartered, washed and dried

85g/3oz ready-to-eat dried apricots, cut into small pieces

2 tbsp nibbed sugar (See Tip)

1 Preheat the oven to180C/350F/Gas 4. Grease and base line a 30x23cm/12x9in roasting tin with greased greaseproof paper. Alternatively, line the tin with non-stick baking paper or greased foil.

2 Place all the ingredients, except the cherries, apricots and nibbed sugar, in a large bowl and beat well for 2 minutes or until well blended. Lightly fold in the cherries and apricots. Transfer to the tin and level the top.

3 Bake for 30–35 minutes, sprinkling over the sugar three-quarters of the way through the cooking time. When cooked, the cake will have shrunk from the sides of the tin and will spring back when pressed in the centre with your fingertips. Cool in the tin, then cut into squares. Lift out using a palette knife.

Nutrition notes per serving: *165 calories, Protein 2g, Carbohydrate 23g, Fat 8g, Saturated fat 5g, Fibre trace, Added sugar 13g, Salt 0.28g.*

TIP

Nibbed sugar is what bakers use on top of Bath buns. Nibs were rough 'shavings' that fell from the early forms of sugar cubes. If you can't find them, use coarsely crushed sugar cubes.

BAKEWELL TART TRAYBAKE

Cuts into 21 squares

4 tbsp raspberry jam

flaked almonds, for sprinkling

FOR THE PASTRY

175g/6oz plain flour

85g/3oz hard margarine, diced

FOR THE SPONGE

115g/4oz soft margarine

115g/4oz caster sugar

175g/6oz self-raising flour

1 tsp baking powder

2 eggs

2 tbsp milk

½ tsp almond essence

1 Preheat the oven to 180C/350F/Gas 4. Make the pastry: rub together the flour and margarine until the mixture resembles fine breadcrumbs. Bind to a dough with two to three tablespoons of cold water. Roll out on a lightly floured surface and line a 30x23cm/12x9in roasting tin, then spread with the jam.

2 Place all the sponge ingredients in a large bowl and beat well for 2 minutes or until well blended. Transfer to the tin, level the top and sprinkle with almonds.

3 Bake for 25 minutes or until the cake has shrunk from the sides of the tin and springs back when pressed in the centre with your fingertips. Leave to cool in the tin, then cut into squares. Lift out using a palette knife.

Nutrition notes per serving: *169 calories, Protein 2g, Carbohydrate 22g, Fat 9g, Saturated fat 2g, Fibre trace, Added sugar 8g, Salt 0.35g.*

Family Cakes

CARROT CAKE ✺

This really is a good recipe. I'm afraid, though, that it sounds rather more healthy than it is.

Cuts into 10 slices

225g/8oz self-raising flour

2 tsp baking powder

140g/5oz light muscovado sugar

55g/2oz walnuts, chopped

115g/4oz carrots, grated (See Tip)

2 ripe bananas, mashed

2 eggs

150ml/¼ pint sunflower oil

FOR THE TOPPING

55g/2oz low-fat soft cheese

55g/2oz soft margarine

115g/4oz icing sugar, sifted

few drops vanilla essence

walnut halves, to decorate

1 Preheat the oven to 180C/350F/Gas 4. Grease and base line a deep 20cm/8in round cake tin with greased greaseproof paper.

2 Place all the cake ingredients in a large bowl and mix well until smooth. Transfer to the tin and level the surface. Bake for 50 minutes–1 hour until the cake is well risen and shrinking away from the sides of the tin. Cool in the tin for a few minutes before turning out, remove the lining paper and leave to cool completely on a wire rack.

3 Make the topping: place all the ingredients, except the walnuts, in a bowl or food processor and mix well until smooth. Spread over the cake, swirling the top with a spatula for a decorative effect, then decorate with walnut halves. Chill a little before serving, or store in the fridge, as the topping is soft.

Nutrition notes per serving: *446 calories, Protein 5g, Carbohydrate 50g, Fat 26g, Saturated fat 4g, Fibre 2g, Added sugar 27g, Salt 0.72g.*

✺ *Freeze in slices, dividing with foil or non-stick baking paper for up to 3 months. Defrost at room temperature before serving.*

TIP

After being grated the carrots should be drained of any excess juice before they are weighed. To speed things up, grate them in a food processor.

BATTENBURG CAKE

You can use home-made or bought almond paste for this famous chequerboard cake.

Cuts into 8 slices

115g/4oz soft margarine

115g/4oz caster sugar

2 large eggs

55g/2oz ground rice

115g/4oz self-raising flour

½ tsp baking powder

few drops almond essence

red food colouring

3–4 tbsp apricot jam, warmed

225g/8oz almond paste (See Tip)

1 Preheat the oven to 160C/325F/Gas 3. Grease and base line a shallow 18cm/7in square cake tin with greased greaseproof paper.

2 Place the margarine, sugar, eggs, ground rice, flour, baking powder and almond essence in a large bowl and beat well for 2 minutes or until smooth. Spoon half the mixture into one half of the cake tin as neatly as possible. Smooth the surface. Add a few drops of red food colouring to the remaining mixture to turn it a deep pink colour, then spoon it into the other half of the tin. Smooth the surface. Try to get the join between the two mixtures as neat as possible.

3 Bake for 35–40 minutes or until the cake is well risen, springy to the touch and has shrunk slightly from the sides of the tin. Turn out, remove the lining paper and leave to cool on a wire rack.

4 Trim the edges of the cake, and cut the square in half down its length to divide the colours. Cut each colour into two equally wide lengthways strips. Use the warm jam to stick the strips of cake together, one plain piece next to one coloured piece, topping with the pieces vice versa, to create a two-tier chequerboard effect. Brush the top of the assembled cake with the jam.

5 Roll out the almond paste into an oblong the length of the cake and sufficiently wide to wrap around it. Invert the cake on to the almond paste, then brush the remaining three sides with jam. Press the almond paste neatly around the cake, arranging the join on one long side. Score the top of the cake with a criss-cross pattern using a sharp knife and crimp the edges with your fingers to seal the join and decorate.

Nutrition notes per serving: *403 calories, Protein 6g, Carbohydrate 55g, Fat 19g, Saturated fat 4g, Fibre 1g, Added sugar 38g, Salt 0.56g.*

TIP

To make almond paste: in a large bowl, mix together 225g/8oz ground almonds with 225g/8oz each of caster sugar and sifted icing sugar. Add four egg yolks or two whole eggs and about six drops of almond essence. Knead together to form a stiff paste. Do not over-knead as this will make the paste oily. Wrap in plastic film and store in the fridge until required. This will make about 675g/1½lb.

CAUTION! This recipe contains raw eggs.

FAST CHRISTMAS CAKE

The simplest and quickest decoration for a Christmas cake is 'instant' royal icing, pulled to a rough peak texture, and a ribbon. You can either buy 'instant' royal icing or, if you want to, you can make your own (See Tip).

Cuts into 16 slices

140g/5oz soft margarine

140g/5oz light muscovado sugar

2 eggs

225g/8oz self-raising flour

400g jar luxury mincemeat

175g/6oz currants

55g/2oz whole almonds, chopped

TO DECORATE

25cm/10in round silver cake board

apricot jam, warmed

675g/1½lb almond paste (page 28)

1 quantity royal icing (See Tip)

length of ribbon

1 Preheat the oven to 160C/325F/Gas 3. Grease and line the base and sides of a deep 20cm/8in round cake tin with greased greaseproof paper (page 62).

2 Place all the cake ingredients in a large bowl and beat well for 1 minute until thoroughly mixed. Transfer to the tin and level the surface.

3 Bake for 1¾ hours or until a skewer inserted into the centre comes out clean and the cake is shrinking from the sides of the tin. Cover with foil after 1 hour if beginning to brown too much. Cool in the tin for about 10 minutes before turning out and cooling completely on a wire rack. Don't remove the lining paper when storing as this helps to keep the cake moist. Wrap the cold cake in a double layer of greaseproof paper, then foil, until needed.

4 Almond-paste the cake a week before icing. Place the cake in the centre of the cake board. Lightly dust a work surface with icing sugar, then roll out the paste to about 5cm/2in larger than the surface of the cake. Brush the cake all over with the jam. Carefully lift the almond paste over the cake with the help of a rolling pin. Gently level and smooth the top of the paste with a rolling pin, then ease the paste down the sides of the cake, smoothing it at the same time. Neatly trim excess off the base, using a sharp knife, then rewrap in grease-proof paper and foil.

5 Spread some of the royal icing thickly over the sides of the cake, smoothing down with a palette knife. Spoon more royal icing on to the top of the cake, then pull the icing on the top into peaks with the back of a spoon. Allow to harden for a few hours before decorating with the ribbon.

Nutrition notes per serving: *619 calories, Protein 7g, Carbohydrate 109g, Fat 20g, Saturated fat 3g, Fibre 2g, Added sugar 77g, Salt 0.45g.*

TIP

To make royal icing: place two egg whites in a large mixing bowl and whisk lightly with a fork until bubbles begin to form on the surface. Add about 250g/9oz sifted icing sugar and four teaspoons fresh lemon juice and beat well with a wooden spoon for about 10 minutes until brilliant white. Gradually stir in 250g/9oz sifted icing sugar until the icing is the correct consistency for piping. Once made, keep the icing covered with a damp cloth to prevent it from drying out. Makes enough to decorate a 20–23cm/8–9in round cake.

DUNDEE CAKE

140g/5oz soft margarine

140g/5oz light muscovado sugar

3 eggs

225g/8oz plain flour

1 tsp baking powder

115g/4oz each of currants, raisins and sultanas

55g/2oz glacé cherries, halved, rinsed and dried

55g/2oz chopped mixed peel

2 tbsp ground almonds

grated rind of 1 orange and 1 lemon

55g/2oz split blanched almonds

1 Preheat the oven to 160C/325F/Gas 3. Grease and base line a deep 20cm/8in round cake tin with greased greaseproof paper.

2 Place the margarine, sugar, eggs, flour and baking powder in a bowl and mix together until well blended, smooth and glossy. Fold in all the remaining ingredients, except the split almonds. Spoon into the tin and level the surface.

3 Arrange the almonds in circles all over the top. Be careful just to rest the almonds on top of the mixture so that they do not sink right into the cake mixture. Bake for 1½–1¾ hours or until the cake is firm and springy to touch and a skewer inserted into the centre comes out clean. Cool in the tin for 30 minutes before removing the lining paper and turning out on to a wire rack to cool completely.

Nutrition notes per serving: *453 calories, Protein 8g, Carbohydrate 64g, Fat 20g, Saturated fat 3g, Fibre 3g, Added sugar 21g, Salt 0.55g.*

TIP

This cake should be kept for a week in an airtight container before eating to improve the flavour.

APPLE AND ALMOND DESSERT CAKE

2 large eggs

225g/8oz caster sugar

225g/8oz self-raising flour

1½ tsp baking powder

½ tsp almond essence

140g/5oz margarine, melted but not hot

315g/11oz prepared cooking apples, cut into fairly thick chunks

25g/1oz flaked almonds

cream, to serve

1 Preheat the oven to 160C/325F/Gas 3. Well grease a 20cm/8in loose-bottomed cake tin.

2 Place the eggs, sugar, flour, baking powder, almond essence and melted margarine in a large bowl. Beat together until evenly mixed. (The mixture will be like a thick sugary batter.)

3 Spread half this mixture over the base of the tin, then top with the apple chunks. (Avoid letting the apples touch the sides of the tin.) Spoon the remaining mixture in blobs over the apples, then sprinkle with the almonds.

4 Bake for 1½ hours or until pale golden and shrinking away from the sides of the tin. Cover lightly with foil if browning too quickly. Cool in the tin for 15 minutes, then turn out and serve warm with cream.

Nutrition notes per serving: *519 calories, Protein 7g, Carbohydrate 73g, Fat 24g, Saturated fat 5g, Fibre 2g, Added sugar 40g, Salt 1.19g.*

SWISS LIME ROLL

This is quick and easy to make and gives a good thick Swiss roll (see opposite page, below). Take care not to overwhisk the eggs and sugar – the mixture should just leave a trail when the beaters are lifted. If you overcook the sponge it will crack when it is rolled up.

Cuts into 10–12 slices

4 large eggs, at room temperature

115g/4oz caster sugar, plus extra for sprinkling

115g/4oz self-raising flour

FOR THE FILLING

grated rind and juice of 1 small lime

300ml/½ pint double cream, lightly whipped

2 tbsp good lemon curd

1 Preheat the oven to 200C/400F/Gas 6. Grease and line a 33x23cm/13x9in Swiss roll tin with greased greaseproof paper. A good way to do this is to turn the tin upside down and mould a piece of greaseproof paper, about 2.5cm/1in larger than the tin, all round over the top. Use to line the tin, folding the corners to give them a good square shape.

2 Whisk the eggs and sugar together in a large bowl until the mixture is light and frothy and the whisk leaves a trail when lifted out. Sift the flour into the mixture, carefully folding it in at the same time.

3 Turn the mixture into the tin and give it a gentle shake so that it finds its own level, making sure that it spreads evenly into the corners. Bake for 10 minutes, or until the sponge is golden brown and begins to shrink from the edges of the tin. Cool in the tin for 5 minutes.

4 Sprinkle a large piece of non-stick baking paper with caster sugar. Invert the sponge on to the sugared paper and carefully remove the lining paper. Trim the sponge edges, if liked. Roll up from a long edge, quickly and turning with the paper inside. Leave to cool.

5 Make the filling: add the lime rind and juice to the cream, then fold in the lemon curd. Carefully unroll the cooled cake, spread evenly with the cream and re-roll, using the paper to help you. Keep chilled until ready to serve.

Nutrition notes per serving for 10: *266 calories, Protein 5g, Carbohydrate 24g, Fat 17g, Saturated fat 10g, Fibre trace, Added sugar 14g, Salt 0.22g.*

VARIATIONS

For an orange Swiss roll, add the finely grated rind of 1 orange to the egg mixture, and mix about two tablespoons orange marmalade with 225g/8oz Greek yogurt for the filling.

For a raspberry (see opposite page, above) or strawberry Swiss roll, fill the basic Swiss roll with 300ml/½ pint whipped cream, and sliced strawberries or whole raspberries or both.

For a smaller Swiss roll, use three eggs and 85g/3oz each of sugar and flour, then bake in a 28x18cm/11x7in tin.

GINGERBREAD

115g/4oz soft margarine

115g/4oz light muscovado sugar

2 eggs

140g/5oz black treacle

140g/5oz golden syrup

225g/8oz plain flour

1 tsp ground ginger

1 tsp ground mixed spice

½ tsp bicarbonate of soda

2 tbsp milk

1   Preheat the oven to 160C/325F/Gas 3. Lightly grease and base line a deep 18cm/7in square cake tin with greased greaseproof paper.

2   Place the margarine, sugar, eggs, treacle and syrup in a bowl and mix together until thoroughly mixed. Sift the flour with the spices and fold into the mixture. Add the bicarbonate of soda to the milk, then stir into the cake mixture. Pour into the tin.

3   Bake for 1 hour. Reduce the oven temperature to 150C/300F/Gas 2 and bake for a further 15–30 minutes until well risen and firm to the touch. Cool in the tin for about 10 minutes, then turn out, remove lining paper and leave to cool completely on a wire rack.

Nutrition notes per serving: *189 calories, Protein 2g, Carbohydrate 32g, Fat 7g, Saturated fat 1g, Fibre trace, Added sugar 20g, Salt 0.36g.*

MADEIRA CAKE

Cuts into 8 slices

175g/6oz butter, softened

175g/6oz caster sugar

225g/8oz self-raising flour

55g/2oz ground almonds

3 large eggs

finely grated rind of 1 lemon

thin slice citron peel (See Tip)

1   Preheat the oven to 180C/350F/Gas 4. Lightly grease and base line a deep 18cm/7in round cake tin with greased greaseproof paper.

2   Place the butter, sugar, flour, ground almonds, eggs and grated lemon rind in a large bowl. Beat well for 1 minute to mix thoroughly, then transfer to the tin.

3   Bake for 30 minutes. Place the citron peel on top of the cake and continue cooking for 30–45 minutes or until a warm skewer inserted into the centre comes out clean. Cool in the tin for 10 minutes, turn out and remove lining paper, then finish cooling on a wire rack.

Nutrition notes per serving: *415 calories, Protein 7g, Carbohydrate 45g, Fat 24g, Saturated fat 12g, Fibre 1g, Added sugar 23g, Salt 0.76g.*

TIP

Citron is a fruit that resembles a lemon but it is larger, longer and greener. Its rind is used in candied form in cookery, and a slice is the traditional decoration for a Madeira cake. Its flesh can be used to make marmalade and, in Corsica, it is also used to make a liqueur.

QUICK FAMILY FRUIT CAKE

A moist fruit cake which keeps well, this is a recipe that was popular after the Second World War. I'm often asked for the boiled fruit cake with condensed milk and no fat that Granny used to make – and this is it – although I do use fat because it is tastier. The surface of the cooked cake does have a slightly shiny appearance; this is quite normal.

Cuts into 8–10 slices

397g can condensed milk

140g/5oz soft margarine

225g/8oz raisins

225g/8oz sultanas

175g/6oz currants

175g/6oz glacé cherries, roughly chopped

225g/8oz self-raising flour

2 tsp ground mixed spice

1 tsp ground cinnamon

2 large eggs

1   Preheat the oven to 150C/300F/Gas 2. Lightly grease and line a deep 18cm/7in round cake tin with greased greaseproof paper (page 62).

2   Pour the condensed milk into a heavy-based pan and add the margarine, fruit and glacé cherries. Place over a low heat until the milk and margarine have melted. Stir well, then simmer for 5 minutes. Remove from the heat and cool for about 10 minutes, stirring occasionally.

3   Place the flour and spices in a large bowl and make a well in the centre, add the eggs and cooled fruit mixture and mix together until well blended. Transfer to the greased tin.

4   Bake for 1¾–2 hours or until the cake is well risen, golden brown and the top feels firm. A skewer inserted into the centre should come out clean. Cool in the tin for 10 minutes, then turn out and leave to cool completely on a wire rack. Don't remove the lining paper when storing as this helps to keep the cake moist. Wrap the cold cake in a double layer of greaseproof paper, then foil, until you are ready to eat it.

Nutrition notes per serving for 8: *678 calories, Protein 11g, Carbohydrate 118g, Fat 22g, Saturated fat 7g, Fibre 3g, Added sugar 35g, Salt 0.92g.*

TIP

If a fruit or Madeira cake (page 36) has a slight dip in the centre when it comes out of the oven, turn on to greaseproof paper on a cooling rack upside down. The action of gravity and the weight of the cake will level the top while it cools. A bit of a cheat, but it works!

WHOLEMEAL GINGER CAKE

Don't be over-generous with the marmalade. Too much marmalade alters the sugar proportion of the recipe and slackens the mixture, which will cause the cake to sink.

175g/6oz soft margarine

350g/12oz golden syrup

125g/4½oz granulated sugar

1½ tbsp orange marmalade

200ml/7fl oz milk

175g/6oz self-raising white flour

1½ tsp ground ginger

1½ tsp ground mixed spice

½ tsp bicarbonate of soda

175g/6oz self-raising brown flour

3 eggs, beaten

FOR THE ICING

3 tbsp fresh lemon juice

225g/8oz icing sugar, sifted

chopped stem ginger, to decorate (optional)

1 Preheat the oven to160C/325F/Gas 3. Grease and base line a 30x23cm/12x9in roasting tin with greased greaseproof paper.

2 Gently heat the margarine, syrup, sugar, marmalade and milk together in a pan until the sugar has dissolved. Cool a little (See Tip).

3 Sift the white flour with the spices and bicarbonate of soda into a bowl. Add the brown flour and mix together. Stir in the melted margarine mixture and the beaten eggs. Stir well to form a smooth batter. Pour into the tin and bake for 1½ hours or until the cake has shrunk slightly from the sides of the tin and is springy to the touch. Turn out, remove the lining paper and cool on a wire rack.

4 Make the icing: mix together the lemon juice and icing sugar and beat until smooth. Spread out evenly over the cake using a palette knife and leave to set. Decorate with stem ginger, if liked. Cut the cake into squares and lift out using a palette knife.

Nutrition notes per serving: *253 calories, Protein 3g, Carbohydrate 45g, Fat 8g, Saturated fat 2g, Fibre trace, Added sugar 32g, Salt 0.56g.*

TIP

Heat the syrup and other ingredients through very gently. If they are too hot when added to the flour the mixture could go lumpy. If it does, you'll have to rub it through a sieve.

ALL-IN-ONE VICTORIA SANDWICH ✽

This must be the best known and loved of all family cakes. The all-in-one method takes away all the hassle of creaming, and ensures success every time.

225g/8oz soft margarine

225g/8oz caster sugar

4 eggs

225g/8oz self-raising flour

2 tsp baking powder

4 tbsp raspberry or strawberry jam

caster sugar, for sprinkling

1 Preheat the oven to 180C/350F/Gas 4. Grease and base line two 20cm/8in sandwich tins with greased greaseproof paper.

2 Place the margarine, sugar, eggs, flour and baking powder in a large bowl and beat well until thoroughly blended. Divide between the tins and level out.

3 Bake for 25 minutes or until the cakes are well risen and the tops spring back when lightly pressed with a finger. Cool in the tins for a few moments, then turn out on to a rack. Very carefully peel off the lining papers, turn the cakes the right way up, then place the tins back over them. This prevents the moisture from evaporating while the cakes are cooling, but doesn't make them soggy. When the cakes are completely cold, sandwich them together with the jam and sprinkle with caster sugar to serve.

Nutrition notes per serving for 8: *478 calories, Protein 6g, Carbohydrate 59g, Fat 26g, Saturated fat 6g, Fibre trace, Added sugar 37g, Salt 1.22g.*

✽ *Whole or sliced sponge cakes freeze well. Wrap in plastic film, foil or polythene bags. Freeze as soon as cold to keep maximum freshness, for up to 3 months.*

VARIATIONS

For an orange or lemon Victoria sandwich, add the finely grated rind of one orange or lemon to the basic mixture and when the cakes are completely cold sandwich them together with four tablespoons orange marmalade or lemon curd. Sprinkle with caster sugar to serve.

For a chocolate Victoria sandwich (see opposite, above), blend two tablespoons sifted cocoa with three tablespoons boiling water in a mixing bowl. Cool, then beat with the cake-mixture ingredients in the basic recipe. (There is no need to reduce the amount of flour.) Sandwich the cakes together and cover the top with white butter cream: blend together 55g/2oz soft margarine, 175g/6oz sifted icing sugar and one tablespoon milk. Decorate with coarsely grated chocolate.

For a coffee Victoria sandwich, beat the eggs in the basic recipe and dissolve two heaped teaspoons of instant coffee in them before beating them with the other cake-mixture ingredients. Sandwich the cakes together with coffee butter cream: add one tablespoon coffee essence, or one heaped teaspoon instant coffee dissolved in one tablespoon hot water, to the white butter cream in the chocolate cake recipe above.

Small Cakes

BUTTERFLY CAKES

These are quick and easy to make and ideal for a children's party.

Makes 18

115g/4oz soft margarine

115g/4oz caster sugar

2 eggs

115g/4oz self-raising flour

1 tsp baking powder

FOR THE BUTTER CREAM

175g/6oz butter, softened

350g/12oz icing sugar, sifted

sifted icing sugar, for dusting

1   Preheat the oven to 200C/400F/Gas 6. Place 18 paper cake cases in bun tins.

2   Place all the ingredients for the cakes in a large bowl and beat well for 2–3 minutes until the mixture is well blended and smooth. Half-fill each paper case with the mixture.

3   Bake for 15–20 minutes until the cakes are well risen and golden brown. Lift the cakes out of the bun tins and cool on a wire rack in the cases.

4   Make the butter cream: beat the butter and icing sugar until well blended. Cut a slice from the top of each cake, then cut each slice in half. Using a small star nozzle, pipe a swirl of butter cream into the centre of each cake. Replace the half slices of cake into the butter cream at an angle to resemble butterfly wings. Dust with icing sugar to serve.

Nutrition notes per serving: *250 calories, Protein 1g, Carbohydrate 32g, Fat 14g, Saturated fat 6g, Fibre trace, Added sugar 27g, Salt 0.46g.*

VARIATIONS

For chocolate butterfly cakes (see opposite, above), replace 25g/1oz of flour in the cake mixture with sifted cocoa, then make a chocolate butter cream: blend two tablespoons of cocoa with three tablespoons of hot water, cool slightly, then beat in 175g/6oz softened butter and 350g/12oz icing sugar until well blended. This chocolate butter cream also looks very attractive on a plain butterfly cake. Dust with icing sugar to serve.

For orange or lemon butterfly cakes, add the finely grated rind of one orange or lemon to the cake mixture, then beat its juice into the butter cream. Dust with icing sugar to serve.

OAT AND SUNFLOWER SQUARES

Makes 16

55g/2oz hard margarine, diced

2 rounded tbsp golden syrup

140g/5oz jumbo oats

55g/2oz sunflower seeds

1 Preheat the oven to 180C/350F/Gas 4. Lightly grease a shallow 18cm/7in square tin.

2 Gently heat the margarine and syrup in a small pan until blended. In a heatproof bowl, mix together the oats and sunflower seeds. Pour over the syrup mixture. Stir thoroughly to mix. Spoon into the tin and press the mixture down well with the back of a spoon.

3 Bake for 20–25 minutes or until golden brown and just firm to the touch. Cut into squares and cool in the tin before carefully lifting out with a palette knife.

Nutrition notes per serving: *88 calories, Protein 2g, Carbohydrate 9g, Fat 5g, Saturated fat 1g, Fibre trace, Added sugar 2g, Salt 0.09g.*

BANANA CHIP BARS

Makes 12

85g/3oz self-raising brown flour

85g/3oz rolled oats

85g/3oz demerara sugar

115g/4oz hard margarine, diced

1 ripe banana, sliced

25g/1oz banana chips

1 Preheat the oven to 180C/350F/Gas 4. Lightly grease a shallow 18cm/7in square tin.

2 Mix together the flour, oats and sugar in a bowl. Rub in the margarine until the mixture resembles breadcrumbs. Spread half the mixture over the base of the tin and arrange the sliced banana on top. Sprinkle over the remaining crumb mixture and press down well. Top with the banana chips.

3 Bake for 25 minutes or until golden brown. Leave in the tin until cold, then cut into bars to serve. Lift out with a palette knife.

Nutrition notes per serving: *169 calories, Protein 2g, Carbohydrate 21g, Fat 9g, Saturated fat 3g, Fibre trace, Added sugar 8g, Salt 0.27g.*

TIP

The banana slices could be replaced with slices of ready-to-eat apricots.

BLUEBERRY MUFFINS

Makes 12

250g/9oz self-raising flour

1 tsp baking powder

55g/2oz soft margarine

85g/3oz caster sugar

175g/6oz fresh blueberries

grated rind of 1 lemon

2 large eggs

225ml/8fl oz milk

1   Preheat the oven to 200C/400F/Gas 6. Lightly grease 12 deep muffin tins if you are using ordinary fairy cake paper cases, as the mixture will rise well above the paper cases, and place the paper cases in the tins (See Tip). You do not need to grease the tins if muffin paper cases are used.

2   Place the flour and baking powder in a large bowl. Rub in the margarine with your fingertips until the mixture resembles fine breadcrumbs. Stir in the sugar, blueberries and lemon rind.

3   Mix together the eggs and milk, then pour the mixture all in one go into the dry ingredients. Mix quickly to blend. The mixture should have a lumpy consistency. Spoon into the paper cases, filling them almost to the top.

4   Bake for 20–25 minutes until well risen, golden and firm to the touch. Cool for a few minutes in the tins, then lift out and cool for a little longer on a wire rack in the cases. Serve warm.

Nutrition notes per serving: *163 calories, Protein 4g, Carbohydrate 25g, Fat 6g, Saturated fat 2g, Fibre trace, Added sugar 7g, Salt 0.45g.*

TIP

Use deep mince-pie tins if you don't have proper muffin tins.

APRICOT SWISS CAKES

Makes 18

85g/3oz icing sugar, sifted

225g/8oz butter, softened

200g/7oz self-raising flour

55g/2oz cornflour

apricot jam, for the filling (See Tip)

sifted icing sugar, for dusting (optional)

1   Preheat the oven to 180C/350F/Gas 4. Place 18 paper cake cases in bun tins.

2   Add the icing sugar to the softened butter and beat well until really soft and fluffy. Stir in the flour and mix until smooth.

3   Spoon the mixture into a large piping bag fitted with a large star nozzle. Pipe circles of the mixture into the base of each paper case until all the mixture is used up.

4   Bake for 15–20 minutes or until pale golden brown. Cool on a wire rack in the cases, then spoon a little jam on to the centre of each cake. Dust lightly with icing sugar, if using.

Nutrition notes per serving: *168 calories, Protein 1g, Carbohydrate 19g, Fat 10g, Saturated fat 7g, Fibre trace, Added sugar 8g, Salt 0.34g.*

TIP

There is nothing to stop you from using any flavour jam for these buttery delights – red jam is, in fact, traditional.

TRADITIONAL ROCK CAKES

Makes 12

225g/8oz self-raising flour (See Tip)

2 tsp baking powder

115g/4oz soft margarine

55g/2oz granulated sugar

115g/4oz mixed dried fruit

55g/2oz currants

1 egg

1 tbsp milk

demerara sugar, for sprinkling

1 Preheat the oven to 200C/400F/Gas 6. Lightly grease two baking trays.

2 Place the flour and baking powder in a large bowl, add the margarine and rub in with your fingertips until the mixture resembles fine breadcrumbs. Stir in the sugar and fruit. Add the egg and milk and mix to a stiff mixture. If dry, add a little more milk.

3 Using two teaspoons, shape the mixture into 12 rough mounds on the baking trays and sprinkle generously with demerara sugar. Bake for 15 minutes or until pale golden brown at the edges. Cool on a wire rack.

Nutrition notes per serving: *200 calories, Protein 3g, Carbohydrate 30g, Fat 9g, Saturated fat 2g, Fibre trace, Added sugar 6g, Salt 0.60g.*

TIP

Use wholemeal self-raising flour if you like, although you may need a little more milk.

ENGLISH MADELEINES

Makes 10

115g/4oz soft margarine

115g/4oz caster sugar

2 eggs

115g/4oz self-raising flour

1 tsp baking powder

2–3 drops vanilla essence

TO DECORATE

4 tbsp raspberry or strawberry jam, sieved

55g/2oz desiccated coconut

5 glacé cherries, halved

1 Preheat the oven to 180C/350F/Gas 4. Lightly grease 10 dariole moulds (these are available from specialist cook shops and department stores) and place circles of greaseproof paper in the bases. Stand the moulds on a baking tray.

2 Place all the cake ingredients in a large bowl and beat for 2 minutes or until the mixture is well blended and smooth. Spoon into the moulds, filling them to about half full.

3 Bake for 20 minutes or until the cakes are well risen and firm to the touch. Leave to cool in the moulds for 5 minutes, then turn on to a wire rack and remove the lining papers.

4 When the cakes are cool, trim the bases so that they stand firmly. Warm the jam in a small pan and spread the coconut out on a plate. Use a fork to spear the cakes to hold them. Brush with the jam, then roll in the coconut to coat. Decorate each madeleine with a halved glacé cherry.

Nutrition notes per serving: *244 calories, Protein 3g, Carbohydrate 29g, Fat 14g, Saturated fat 5g, Fibre 1g, Added sugar 19g, Salt 0.50g.*

Scones & Teabreads

SCONES

Scones piled high with clotted cream and strawberry jam are a classic essential for a proper afternoon tea. The secret of good scones is not to handle them too much before baking, and to make the mix on the wet, sticky side. Butter gives the best flavour to scones, but margarine can be used if you prefer. If you have any left over, cut in half and toast them for breakfast or freeze them, then refresh in a moderate oven before serving.

Makes 12

225g/8oz self-raising flour
2 tsp baking powder
55g/2oz butter, diced
25g/1oz caster sugar
1 egg
milk, to mix

1 Preheat the oven to 220C/425F/Gas 7. Lightly grease two baking trays.

2 Place the flour and baking powder in a bowl, then rub in the butter with your fingertips until the mixture resembles fine breadcrumbs. Stir in the sugar.

3 Break the egg into a measuring jug, then make up to 150ml/¼pint with milk. Stir the egg and milk into the flour – you may not need it all – and mix to a soft but sticky dough. Turn out on to a lightly floured surface, knead lightly, then roll out to 1cm/½in thick.

4 Cut into rounds with a fluted 5cm/2in cutter and place on the baking trays. Brush the tops with a little extra milk or left-over egg and milk mixture and bake for 10 minutes or until the scones are pale golden brown. Cool on a wire rack. Eat as fresh as possible. Wrap in a clean tea towel after baking to keep moist.

Nutrition notes per serving: *117 calories, Protein 2g, Carbohydrate 17g, Fat 5g, Saturated fat 3g, Fibre trace, Added sugar 2g, Salt 0.49g.*

 Pack the cooked, cooled scones in plastic bags, seal, label and freeze for up to 6 months. Defrost in the bags for 2–3 hours at room temperature, then refresh in a 200C/400F/Gas 6 preheated oven for 3 minutes.

VARIATIONS

For brown scones (see opposite), use wholemeal self-raising flour instead of white. You may need to add a little more liquid.

For fruit scones (see opposite), simply add 55g/2oz mixed dried fruit to the basic mixture.

CRUNCHY TOP LEMON LOAVES ❄

Each loaf cuts into 6–8 slices

115g/4oz soft margarine

175g/6oz self-raising flour

1 tsp baking powder

175g/ 6oz caster sugar

2 large eggs

4 tbsp milk

finely grated rind of 1 lemon

FOR THE TOPPING

juice of 1 lemon

115g/4oz granulated sugar

1 Preheat the oven to 180C/350F/Gas 4. Lightly grease and line two 450g/1lb loaf tins with a strip of greased greaseproof paper wide enough to cover the two long sides and the base of the tin.

2 Place all the loaf ingredients in a large bowl and beat well for 2 minutes. Divide between the tins and level the surfaces. Bake for 35–40 minutes, or until the loaves spring back when their surfaces are lightly pressed with a finger and they have shrunk slightly from the sides of the tins.

3 Meanwhile, make the topping: place the lemon juice and sugar in a small bowl and stir to mix. Spread this mixture over the baked loaves while they are still hot, then leave to cool completely in the tins. Turn out when cold and remove the lining papers.

Nutrition notes per serving for 6: *232 calories, Protein 3g, Carbohydrate 37g, Fat 9g, Saturated fat 2g, Fibre trace, Added sugar 25g, Salt 0.50g.*

❄ *Freeze whole or in slices wrapped in foil, plastic film or in a polythene bag for up to 3 months. Defrost at room temperature.*

BORROWDALE TEABREAD ❄ Ⓕ

Cuts into 18 slices

115g/4oz sultanas

115g/4oz currants

115g/4oz raisins

300ml/10fl oz strong tea, strained

225g/8oz dark muscovado sugar

1 egg

275g/10oz self-raising brown flour

1 Place the fruit in a bowl with the tea and leave, covered, overnight. Preheat the oven to 160C/325F/Gas 3. Grease and base line a 900g/2lb loaf tin with greased greaseproof paper.

2 Mix together the sugar and eggs until light and fluffy. Add the flour with the soaked fruits and any remaining liquid and mix thoroughly. Spoon into the tin and level the surface.

3 Bake for 1½ hour or until a skewer inserted into the centre comes out clean. Cool in the tin, remove the lining paper, then slice and serve with butter.

Nutrition notes per serving: *155 calories, Protein 3g, Carbohydrate 37g, Fat 1g, Saturated fat trace, Fibre 1g, Added sugar 13g, Salt 0.03g.*

❄ *Freeze whole or in slices wrapped in foil, plastic film or in a polythene bag for up to 3 months. Defrost at room temperature.*

TIP

If you prefer you can make two 450g/1lb loaves. Shorten the cooking time to 30–40 minutes.

ICED APRICOT FRUIT LOAF ✹

Cuts into 12 slices

3 large eggs

85g/3oz glacé cherries, quartered, washed and dried (See Tip)

175g/6oz self-raising flour

115g/4oz soft margarine

115g/4oz light muscovado sugar

115g/4oz ready-to-eat dried apricots, chopped

140g/5oz sultanas

FOR THE ICING

115g/4oz icing sugar, sifted

1 tbsp apricot jam

2 ready-to-eat dried apricots, chopped, to decorate

1 Preheat the oven to 160C/325F/Gas 3. Lightly grease and base line a 900g/2lb loaf tin with greased greaseproof paper.

2 Break the eggs into a large bowl, then add the remaining loaf ingredients. Beat well until the mixture is smooth, then transfer to the tin and level the top.

3 Bake for 1 hour 10 minutes or until the loaf is golden, firm to the touch and shrinking away from the sides of the tin. A fine skewer inserted should come out clean. Cool in the tin for 10 minutes, then turn out, remove the lining paper and cool completely on a wire rack.

4 Make the icing: place the icing sugar in a bowl, heat the jam with one table-spoon of water until the jam melts, then pour on to the icing sugar. Mix to a smooth spreading consistency, then spoon over the top of the loaf. Sprinkle the chopped apricots down the centre of the loaf, to decorate.

Nutrition notes per serving: *289 calories, Protein 4g, Carbohydrate 49g, Fat 10g, Saturated fat 2g, Fibre 1g, Added sugar 25g, Salt 0.40g.*

✱ *Freeze undecorated for up to 3 months wrapped in foil, plastic film or in a polythene bag. Defrost at room temperature, then ice and decorate.*

TIP

Glacé cherries contain a lot of moisture and syrup so they need to be washed and dried so that they don't sink to the bottom of the loaf.

BANANA AND HONEY TEABREAD ✹

Cuts into 12 slices

225g/8oz self-raising flour

¼ tsp freshly grated nutmeg

115g/4oz soft margarine, diced

225g/8oz ripe bananas, mashed

115g/4oz caster sugar

grated rind of 1 lemon

2 large eggs

6 tbsp thick honey

FOR THE TOPPING

2 tbsp thick honey

nibbed sugar (See Tip, page 24) or crushed sugar cubes, for sprinkling

1 Preheat the oven to 180C/350F/Gas 4. Lightly grease and base line a 900g/2lb loaf tin with greased greaseproof paper.

2 Place the flour and nutmeg in a large bowl and rub in the margarine until the mixture resembles fine breadcrumbs. Stir in all the remaining loaf ingredients and beat until thoroughly mixed, then transfer to the tin and level the top.

3 Bake for 1¼ hours or until a fine skewer inserted into the centre comes out clean. Cover loosely with foil towards the end of cooking if browning too quickly. Cool slightly in the tin, then turn out, remove the lining paper and leave to cool completely on a wire rack .

4 Make the topping: gently warm the honey in a small pan, brush over the top of the teabread and sprinkle with nibbed sugar.

Nutrition notes per serving: *242 calories, Protein 3g, Carbohydrate 39g, Fat 9g, Saturated fat 3g, Fibre trace, Added sugar 20g, Salt 0.41g.*

✱ *Freeze without the topping for up to 3 months wrapped in foil, plastic film or in a polythene bag. Defrost at room temperature, then add the topping.*

Children's Favourites

JUMBLES

140g/5oz soft margarine

140g/5oz caster sugar

few drops vanilla essence

finely grated rind of 1 lemon

1 egg

350g/12oz plain flour

clear honey, to glaze

demerara sugar, for sprinkling

1 Preheat the oven to 190C/375F/Gas 5. Lightly grease three baking trays.
2 Place all the ingredients, except the honey and demerara sugar, in a bowl and work together by hand until a dough is formed. (This can be done in a food processor or with an electric mixer if you prefer.) Divide into 32 pieces. Roll each piece into a 10cm/4in long strip, then twist into an 's' shape. Place on the baking trays and chill for 30 minutes.
3 Bake for 10–15 minutes until pale golden and remove from the oven. Increase the oven temperature to 230C/450F/Gas 8 and while the jumbles are still warm brush with honey and sprinkle with sugar. Return to the oven for 2–3 minutes until the sugar has caramelized. Cool on a wire rack.

Nutrition notes per serving: *93 calories, Protein 1g, Carbohydrate 14g, Fat 4g, Saturated fat 1g, Fibre trace, Added sugar 5g, Salt 0.10g.*

TIP

It is usual to shape this mixture into an 's' but, of course, you can shape it into any letter or number of your choice.

MINI JAMMY BUNS

Makes 24

225g/8oz self-raising flour

¼ tsp ground mixed spice

55g/2oz soft margarine

115g/4oz caster sugar

1 egg, beaten

3–4 tbsp milk

2–3 tbsp blackcurrant jam

granulated sugar, for sprinkling

1 Preheat the oven to 200C/400F/Gas 6. Lightly grease two baking trays.
2 Place the flour and spice in a bowl and rub in the margarine with your fingertips until the mixture resembles fine breadcrumbs. Stir in the sugar.
3 Mix together the egg and milk and stir into the mixture, adding sufficient to make a stiff dough. Divide into 24 pieces and roll each piece into a smooth ball. Make a hole in the centre of each ball using the handle of a wooden spoon and put about a quarter of a teaspoon of jam into each one. Place the balls, jam-side up, on the baking sheets and sprinkle with granulated sugar.
4 Bake for 10 minutes or until pale golden brown. Lift off the baking sheets and cool a little on a wire rack before eating warm.

Nutrition notes per serving: *75 calories, Protein 1g, Carbohydrate 13g, Fat 2g, Saturated fat 1g, Fibre trace, Added sugar 6g, Salt 0.14g.*

TOFFEE AND MARSHMALLOW SQUARES

Makes 20 squares

115g/4oz hard margarine

115g/4oz marshmallows

115g/4oz dairy toffees

200g/7oz rice krispies

1 Place the margarine, marshmallows and toffees in a heavy-based pan and heat gently for about 5 minutes or until the mixture is melted and smooth.

2 Place the rice krispies in a heatproof bowl, pour over the toffee mixture and stir to mix. Spoon into a lightly greased 30x23cm/12x9in tin and press flat. Leave in a cool place to set until quite firm, then cut into squares. Lift out with a palette knife.

Nutrition notes per serving: *119 calories, Protein 1g, Carbohydrate 17g, Fat 6g, Saturated fat 2g, Fibre trace, Added sugar 8g, Salt 0.49g.*

MELTING MOMENTS

Makes 36

225g/8oz soft margarine

175g/6oz golden caster sugar

2 egg yolks

few drops vanilla essence

280g/10oz self-raising flour

55g/2oz rolled oats

9 glacé cherries, quartered (optional)

1 Preheat the oven to 190C/375F/Gas 5. Lightly grease two baking trays.

2 Place the margarine, sugar, egg yolks, vanilla essence and flour in a mixing bowl and mix together to form a soft dough.

3 Divide into 36 portions, form each piece into a ball and roll it in the oats to cover. Flatten the balls slightly and top each one with a quartered cherry, if liked. Place on the baking trays and bake for 20 minutes or until golden. Cool on the baking trays for a few moments before lifting on to a wire rack to cool completely.

Nutrition notes per serving: *103 calories, Protein 1g, Carbohydrate 13g, Fat 6g, Saturated fat 1g, Fibre trace, Added sugar 6g, Salt 0.20g.*

TIP

Ensure the biscuits stay oven-fresh crisp. Leave to go completely cold before storing in a tin, and never store in the same tin as a cake – they will absorb its moisture and go soft and soggy.

Secrets of Success

Instructions are included in individual recipes, but a few extra tips are gathered together here.

PREPARING AND LINING TINS

To grease tins, use a pastry brush to brush melted fat evenly over the tin (I find white vegetable fat best).

BASES

Whatever the shape of the tin, place the base on the greaseproof paper, draw round it in pencil, then cut just inside the pencil line. If you do a lot of baking it's worth cutting out several bases at once and storing them flat in a polythene bag. You can also buy them ready cut. Loose-bottomed tins do not have to be lined unless specified; simply grease the base and sides.

SIDES

For rich fruit cakes it is necessary to line both the base and sides. Cut a strip (or two if necessary) of grease-proof paper long enough to reach around the tin and overlap slightly, and deep enough to extend about 2.5cm/1in above the top of the tin. Fold the bottom edge of the strip up by about 2.5cm/1in, creasing it firmly. Lift up the folded edge and cut slanting lines into this narrow strip at regular intervals. Fit this strip into the greased tin – the snipped edge will ensure it lies flat – then place the base disc over the top. Grease well.

QUICK TIN LINING

Turn the tin to be lined upside down and mould a piece of foil over the top. Use this to line the tin, then grease it well. This is useful, too, in loose-bottomed tins if a mixture is runny and might seep out.

BAKING

Cook cakes in the centre of the oven unless otherwise specified. Never open the oven door or move the cake during the initial stages of baking, as both these actions will make the cake sink in the middle. Don't cram the oven, even if it is a fan oven, as there needs to be a good circulation of air around the tins. Remember two or more cakes cooked in the same oven at once will take longer to cook than one. If anything looks as though it might be browning too much too early, place a sheet of foil loosely over the top.

STORING

If cakes are not to be eaten immediately a freezer is the best place to store them, although some icings may weep a little on defrosting. Cakes can be open-frozen on the lid, before being wrapped and stored in the freezer. Alternatively, wrap well in plastic film or foil.
If you are not freezing your cake, keep it fresh in a large airtight biscuit tin. Place the cake on the inside of the lid, then place the bulk of the tin over the top. Otherwise the cake could be difficult to extract!

INDEX